HOW TO LOOK AFTER YOUR

KITTEN

WIDE EYED EDITIONS

Wide Eyed Editions
www.wideeyededitions.com

How To Look After Your Kitten © Aurum Press Ltd 2015
Text © Helen Piers Estate 2015

First published in the United States in 2015 by Wide Eyed Editions
an imprint of Quarto Inc.,
276 Fifth Avenue, Suite 206, New York, NY 10001.
www.wideeyededitions.com

ISBN 978-1-84780-698-7

The illustrations were created digitally.
Set in Fugue, A Thousand Years, First Time in Forever and Sue Ellen Francisco

Designed by Nicola Price
Edited by Emily Hawkins and Jenny Broom
Published by Rachel Williams

Printed in Shenzhen, Guangdong, China

1 3 5 7 9 8 6 4 2

CONTENTS

KITTENS AND CATS AS PETS

Some four thousand years ago, cats were first brought into people's homes, probably to help catch mice and rats.

Nowadays, most people enjoy pet cats for company. They are not expensive to care for and they are very clean: a cat spends hours grooming itself and is easy to house-train. Cats have an independent nature. They like to come and go as they please. They won't obey commands, as a dog will, and you can't train them to do tricks or take them for walks. But they make excellent pets—they can be let outside and trusted to find their own way home, they will often go out of their way to seek your company, and they will return every bit of affection they are given. They will ask to be stroked and petted, then will show their contentment by purring.

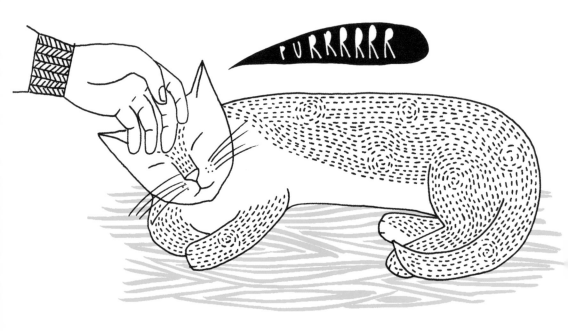

PURRRRRR

CONSIDER THESE THINGS BEFORE YOU ADOPT A KITTEN...

What does it cost to care for a cat?

A cat is not expensive to care for, but you will need to buy its food and cat litter. You will also have to pay for vaccinations, regular vet visits, and probably some other vet's fees (to spay or neuter, for instance) during its life.

Does a cat need a lot of looking after?

Cats need to be fed twice a day, have plenty of fresh water, and have their litter box emptied daily. Long-haired cats require frequent grooming. A cat can be left on its own without getting too lonely during the day, but you can't leave it to fend for itself when you are on vacation. You'll need to send it to a good cattery, or ask a friend to visit twice a day to feed it and change the water and litter.

Are some people allergic to cats?

Some people get hay fever, asthma or skin rashes from cat dander, so keeping a cat in the same house as them would be difficult.

Can a cat be kept indoors all the time?

Choose your cat carefully if your house has no yard. While some cats might miss an outdoor life, other breeds are better suited to living indoors.

THE RIGHT CAT FOR YOU

It's important to choose the right kind of cat for your home and family. If you don't have a lot of spare time for grooming, for example, then a long-haired cat may not be a good choice.

AWW, CUTE!

Cat or kitten?

Both kittens and older cats can make great pets. Kittens are sweet and fun new members of the family and you should be able to train them easily if you start when they are young. However, they take quite a lot of work: you will need to kitten-proof your house and put time into training.

With an adult cat, you know exactly what you're getting, and there are many adult cats out there in need of a loving home. A possible disadvantage of adopting an adult cat is that it may have some behavior problems—such as not using a litter box—that might be hard to correct. However, a good rescue center will tell you about any problems before you adopt.

Male or female?

Both can be equally affectionate. Females tend to stay at home more, while males — before they're neutered — will roam the neighborhood and may stay away for several days when looking for a mate. Many vets recommend that you spay or neuter your cat (see page 30).

Pedigree or domestic?

A pedigree, or pure-bred, cat is one whose ancestors were all the same breed. Pure-bred kittens are expensive to buy, but some people choose them because they like the look and character of a particular breed.

A domestic cat is a mixture of breeds, and except for its mother, its ancestry is often unknown. Most pet cats are domestic. They are usually clever and independent, and suffer fewer health problems than pedigrees.

Long-haired or short-haired?

Long-haired cats are very beautiful, but need frequent grooming to keep their coats in good condition.

DIFFERENT BREEDS OF CAT

There are more than eighty different breeds of pedigree cat.
Here are a few of the most popular . . .

Burmese

Short-haired, sleek, athletic,
brave, boisterous

Persian

Long-haired, gentle, placid,
affectionate, soft musical voice

Siamese

Short-haired; distinctive dark mask,
ears, socks and tail; blue eyes, very
talkative, strong personality

Birman

Long-haired, active, playful, gentle, very responsive to training; born pure white at birth, its markings come in later

Ragdoll

Long-haired, large, affectionate and placid; will often go limp and floppy when picked up

British shorthair

Large, affectionate and cuddly; makes an excellent family pet

American shorthair

Affectionate and playful, robust and healthy

GETTING READY FOR YOUR KITTEN

Before you bring a kitten or adult cat home, there are a few things you need to get ready to make sure she will be comfortable.

Cat bed

You can either buy one or make one from an old cardboard box lined with newspaper. Keep it in a warm, quiet corner away from drafts. You could line the bed with an old sweatshirt—your scent might comfort the kitten.

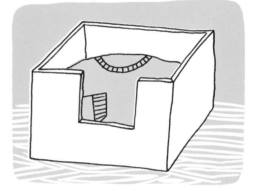

Food and water bowls

These should be stainless steel or ceramic. Make sure you wash them every day to keep them clean.

Litter box, cat litter, and scoop

This is where your kitten will go to the bathroom (see page 19). Keep this clean by washing it once a week with soap and water; your kitten won't like using a smelly, dirty box.

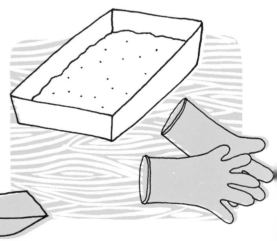

Cat carrier

You'll need this to bring your kitten home and for trips to the vet. Try to get your kitten used to the carrier from a young age, because if she only sees it when going to the vet she might become scared of it!

Grooming supplies

Long-haired cats need daily grooming.

Toys

Your kitten will love playing—it is important to keep her fit and to help her develop.

KITTEN-PROOFING YOUR HOME

Kittens learn about objects by chewing them and don't always know when something could be dangerous, so make sure you make your home as safe as possible.

- Keep harmful household chemicals—for instance, cleaning products, medicines, and poisons—in a locked cabinet.

- Keep all windows and doors shut (your kitten should not be allowed outside for the first few months).

- Use covered trash cans in the kitchen and bathroom.

- Keep the toilet lid closed so your kitten can't fall in.

- Always keep the doors of the fridge, oven, microwave, washer, and dryer closed so the kitten can't crawl inside.

- Make sure there are no electrical cables that could be chewed, or open chimneys that a kitten could climb up.

- Keep your kitten away from plants that could be toxic (for example, lilies).

CHOOSING A KITTEN

To find a new kitten, try asking friends who have cats—they may know of kittens that need homes.

You could also ask at an animal shelter or a veterinarian. If you want a pedigree cat, you will need to find a registered breeder who is a member of the breed club for whichever type you have chosen. Make sure you don't visit more than one breeder on the same day; this will keep you from carrying infections between the kittens.

Which kitten?

When choosing a kitten, it's a good idea to see the whole litter and meet the mother first: the mother's personality and behavior will give you an idea of what the kittens will be like when they are fully grown. Take time choosing a kitten. One that approaches you fearlessly may be a better choice than one—however pretty—who is too frightened to come close.

 If you are choosing a kitten from a litter, ask to hold each kitten in turn to help you decide which you feel happiest with.

THERE ARE SOME IMPORTANT QUESTIONS TO ASK WHEN CHOOSING A KITTEN...

Is it healthy?

A healthy kitten will be lively and playful. Its eyes should be bright, clear, and not runny; its coat should be clean and glossy with no bare or thin patches. There should be no sign of diarrhea and no black specks or dark wax inside its ears—a symptom of ear mites.

How old is it?

Between twelve and sixteen weeks is best. By then the kitten will be weaned onto solid food and independent enough to leave its mother. Pedigree kittens will stay with the breeder until they are thirteen weeks old.

What food is it used to?

Ask what food the kitten has been given, and how often. You should stick to the same food for the first two weeks. If you wish to change its diet later, do so gradually.

Has it been vaccinated?

The breeder, shelter, or store should supply a vaccination certificate signed by a vet.

Does it have a pedigree certificate?

A pure-bred kitten should have a certificate giving its date of birth and ancestry.

Is it house-trained?

Ask if it has been using a litter box and what kind of litter it is used to.

Is it used to people?

If your house is noisy and busy, make sure the kitten will feel at home in a similar environment.

Make sure you spend time with a kitten and ask lots of questions before you decide to bring it home.

TAKING YOUR KITTEN HOME

The journey

If you're traveling by car, make sure you safely secure the cat carrier. Your kitten may cry, because being in a car will be a strange new experience, but don't open the carrier to comfort her—she may panic and leap out. Instead, try talking soothingly to her.

Home, sweet home

At home, wait quietly before opening the carrier. Later, gently lift out your kitten, then let her find her water, bed, and litter box (you may want to use litter from the breeder, pet store, or shelter).

She will be nervous, so let her explore while you sit quietly and watch. She may run off and hide, but be patient and wait for her to come out. It's better to keep your kitten in one room for a day or two before you give her the run of the house.

A good night's sleep

Your kitten may be lonely the first few nights. Help her feel less alone by putting a warm hot-water bottle and a quietly ticking clock—well wrapped—in her bed. These will mimic the warmth and heartbeat of her mother.

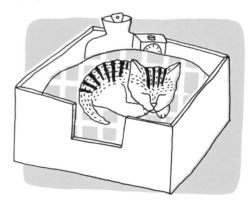

Settling in

When your kitten is well rested, you can introduce her new human family. Everyone should sit on the floor and touch the kitten only if she approaches. When you stroke her, run your hand from her head along her back (some cats don't like having their tummies tickled).

The next few weeks will be an important time for your kitten, as she gets to know and trust you. Be patient and gentle, and don't expect her to play all the time. Kittens sleep a lot, so there will be times when she would rather snooze than play.

Picking up your kitten

The best way to pick up a kitten is to slip one hand under it, just behind its front legs, and let it sit on the other hand. Don't pick it up by the scruff of the neck, and never grasp it tightly with both hands around its stomach, or grab hold of it by the tail.

YES!

NO

PLAY TIME

Until he is about five months old, your kitten will spend nearly all his waking time playing. This is the way he learns about the world.

You can have great fun playing with him or just watching. Even grown-up cats will still want to play sometimes. Just as in humans, exercise is important to stay healthy.

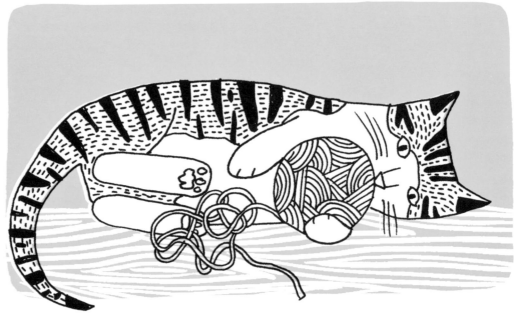

Toys everywhere!

You can give your kitten a wand with ribbon or feathers to play with, soft toys, or crumpled-up paper. And he's sure to find other toys for himself! Make sure that he doesn't play with anything sharp or small enough to swallow.

 Be very careful that your cat doesn't get hold of yarn or thread with a needle attached.

Keeping it fun

Cats can get bored, so keep yours interested by swapping his toys every few days. Sprinkle catnip (a cat–friendly herb) on a toy to see your cat go wild!

Hunter-in-training

Cats are hunters by nature and when a kitten plays it is usually pretending to hunt or fight. Dangle something in front of your kitten and he will stretch out a paw and try to catch it. He will bring his toys to life by patting or tossing them around so he can stalk and chase them.

TRAINING YOUR KITTEN

While your kitten is young, you can train him how you want him to behave.

It's hard to change the habits of an adult cat, so get started early. A kitten doesn't know when he's doing something wrong, and will not understand if you punish him. When training, it's important to remember that you are teaching your kitten good habits, not punishing him.

Forbidden places

There may be rooms your kitten isn't allowed in, or cupboards he could get shut inside by mistake. He may want to jump on tables where there is food. He has to learn that these places are out of bounds.

Teach him by picking him up as soon as he goes to a forbidden place. Hiss and say "No!" firmly. Don't overdo it; you don't want to scare him—only startle him a little so he learns to avoid that place.

Clawing furniture

In the same way, you can train your kitten not to claw furniture and carpets. However, all cats need something to scratch on to keep their claws in good condition.

The best thing is to get a scratching post. It should be sturdy and tall enough to let your kitten stretch out full length.

Using a litter box

Position your cat's litter box away from his food and water in a quiet, safe place: cats need to feel protected and private when going to the bathroom. Your kitten has to learn that the litter box is the only place he's allowed to go to the bathroom. If he starts to go anywhere else, pick him up at once, hissing, then take him to the box. If he has already made a mess, clean up the mess wearing rubber gloves. Then, spray the place with vinegar to cover the smell; this will discourage the kitten from using the same area again.

If you want your cat to go to the bathroom outside when he's older, mix some earth into the cat litter and leave the tray by the yard door. Once your cat is allowed out on his own, move the box outside and keep it there until he finds places in the yard to use instead.

TRAINING TIPS

- Be consistent. Don't keep your kitten from jumping on a table one day and let him the next.

- Don't slap your kitten. He won't understand, and you might hurt him.

- Don't discipline your kitten after he's misbehaved. Instead, try to catch him in the act.

- A cat won't use a dirty litter box. Scoop out poop as soon as you see it and make sure you wash the box regularly.

- Always wear rubber gloves and wash your hands after handling the litter box; cat poop can carry harmful parasites.

CAT TALK

Like people, cats have different personalities and moods. The more time you spend with your cat, the better you will get at understanding her body language. Soon your cat will be able to talk to you without saying a word!

Relaxed

You'll know when your cat is at her most relaxed: she will be sitting or lying down with her eyes half-closed, purring.

Friendly

To spot a friendly cat, look for forward-pointing ears, fanned whiskers, and a tail held high; then listen for a friendly meow.

Annoyed

Beware of a cat with a twitching tail, ears back, and enlarged pupils— these are all signs that she's feeling irritated.

Playful

If your cat is rolling on the ground with her tail curled, ears forward, and whiskers fanned, then she's probably ready to play!

MEOOOOW!

Your cat will make lots of different noises, each one means something different.

 Meow: Can mean many things, including "Hello!", "Feed me" or "Open the door now!"

 Purring: A sign of a happy, contented cat.

 Growling or hissing: A sign of anger or fear.

 Howling or yowling: May mean that your cat is in distress, perhaps stuck in a cupboard or in pain. If your cat hasn't been neutered yet (see page 30), these sounds can be part of normal mating behavior.

 Chattering and twittering: Your cat may make these strange sounds if she's sitting at the window watching birds or other animals outside. They may be a sign of excitement or of frustration that she can't get to the prey.

Aggressive

Watch out for flattened ears, an arched back, raised hair along the spine, a rigid tail, enlarged pupils, and hissing or growling— this cat is in the mood for a fight.

Frightened or startled

A nervous or startled cat will hold her tail low and flatten her ears and whiskers; she may also hiss or growl.

GOING OUTDOORS

Your cat has the best of two worlds. Indoors, he can enjoy comfort and human company; while outdoors, he can do things that are natural for a wild cat to do: hunting, defending his territory, and basking in the sun.

When can my cat go outside?

Keep your kitten inside for two weeks after finishing his first course of vaccinations (usually at thirteen or fourteen weeks). If you want him to explore the yard, you must stay with him for the first few months. Your cat must not be allowed out alone until after he or she has been neutered or spayed (see page 30) around five or six months old.

Cat door

You may choose to have a cat door installed so your cat can come and go as he pleases. Teach your cat to use it by propping it open and tempting him through with some food. To stop other cats from coming in, you can get cat doors that open only when they detect a special signal from your own cat's collar.

Hunting and fighting

Try not to be upset if your cat brings you a creature it has caught. It's a natural instinct for a cat to hunt, and by bringing you his catch, he is showing that he feels a family bond with you. Most cat fights are about territory. Cats will mark out their own piece of neighborhood and defend it fiercely. The best way to break up a fight is to clap and make a lot of noise.

Straying

Sometimes cats can't find their way home. If your cat goes missing, put up "Lost" signs and ask at local animal shelters. Don't give up hope: some cats have been found after they've been missing for several months.

You should put a collar on your cat with an ID tag listing your phone number. You must choose a quick-release collar, so the cat can wriggle out of it if it gets caught on something. It's a good idea to get your cat microchipped by a vet, so if he gets lost he can be returned to you.

Avoiding dangers

Some people keep their cats inside at night, when they are more likely to get into fights or be run over.

If you live near a busy road, you could encourage your cat to come inside during rush hours by feeding him at these times. You may also want to give him a fluorescent collar to help drivers see him.

FEEDING YOUR KITTEN

At first, you should feed your kitten the same diet he was given by the breeder, pet store, or shelter, to avoid upsetting his stomach.

If you want to change his diet, do this gradually over ten days by mixing in some new food with the old food, increasing the proportion of new food every day.

Kittens have small stomachs so they need to be fed little and often. They can burn up to three times more calories than adult cats, so they need special food. High-quality kitten food is designed to give kittens all the nutrients they need. This can either be wet (canned or in pouches) or dry.

Don't interrupt your kitten while he's eating!

It's hard to say exactly how much food to give because all cats are different, but follow the guidelines on the container. If your kitten doesn't finish what you put down for him, then start to give less. A cat will ask for more if he's hungry.

Feed your kitten in the same place and at the same times each day,. because cats are creatures of habit. Choose a quiet place, away from the litter tray. Don't bother him while he's eating, and take away any wet food that has not been eaten after half an hour.

HOW OFTEN SHOULD I FEED MY KITTEN?

🐾 Up to 4 months (after weaning): 4 meals a day

🐾 4–6 months: 3 meals a day

🐾 6 months on: 2 meals a day

Feeding an adult cat

You should gradually switch to a complete adult cat food when your cat is fully grown—usually at about a year old.

When your cat is seven or eight, he might become less active and your vet may advise that you gradually switch to a different cat food designed especially for older cats.

Drinking

Always leave a bowl of water out for your cat—especially if you feed him dry food. If he doesn't seem eager to drink, try a bigger bowl: some cats don't like their whiskers touching the sides. Don't give cats milk, as it can cause diarrhea.

Choose a high-quality brand of complete cat food suitable for your type of cat.

Treats

Most cat treats are designed for full-grown cats, so don't give them to your kitten. Giving your adult cat an occasional treat by hand is a good way of strengthening the bond between you, but make sure it is suitable for your cat. Some foods can be harmful: onions, chocolate, grapes, and raisins, for example.

GROOMING

Cats are very particular about keeping clean and kittens soon learn to groom themselves.

Grooming your kitten is a lovely way to bond with her and will also give you a chance to make sure she is healthy. Start grooming her from a young age so she learns to enjoy it. First, give her a gentle stroke, then begin softly brushing once she is relaxed.

Things to check

Grooming your cat gives you a chance to look for lumps, bumps, or scratches that might need to be checked by a vet. You should also check that her ears are clean inside, her claws aren't split or growing too long, and that there are no bare patches in her coat. All of these would need treatment.

Hairballs

As the seasons change, your cat will shed her coat more than usual. You should groom her well when she is shedding, or she might swallow too many hairs. These could make hairballs in her stomach, which may cause an uncomfortable blockage.

Long-haired cats

A long-haired cat needs brushing and combing regularly — daily if possible. First, tease out any tangles with a wide-toothed comb. Try sprinkling talcum powder onto knots and coaxing them out with your fingers. Then, brush her all over. The best way to get rid of loose hairs is to brush the opposite way from the direction the hair grows. Never use scissors to remove matted hair, as you could cut your cat's skin.

Short-haired

Long-haired

Short-haired cats

Short-haired cats should be groomed once a week or so to get rid of loose hairs and keep the skin healthy. However, when your cat is shedding more than usual, it's worth grooming her more regularly to keep hairballs from forming. Brush her gently with a soft brush from head to tail, being very careful around the head.

KEEPING YOUR CAT HEALTHY

There are a few important things you need to do to make sure your cat stays healthy.

If she seems sick, is not eating, or has diarrhea for more than a few days, don't put off taking her to the vet. Even if she seems well, you should take her to the vet once a year for a check-up and vaccination.

SIGNS OF ILLNESS

Keep an eye out for these tell-tale signs that your cat isn't well:

 Eating less than normal

 Drinking more than usual

 Vomiting

 Diarrhea

 Difficulty peeing or pooping

 A dull and "spiky" coat

 Difficulty breathing

 Dull or runny eyes

 A runny nose

Not grooming

The vet will show you how to clean your kitten's ears and clip her claws.

Vaccination

Your kitten must be vaccinated against cat flu and other illnesses. She will need two injections a few weeks apart (usually at nine and twelve weeks), plus an annual booster.

Scratches

If your cat is scratched in a fight, you should clean the wound by bathing it in warm water (boiled first then allowed to cool) mixed with a bit of salt. You should take your cat to the vet, who will check the wound for infection and may have to give stitches.

Parasites and fleas

Tiny parasites—often called worms—can live inside a cat's intestines. Ask your vet for advice on how to treat them.

De-flea your cat regularly, even if you don't think she has fleas on her. A vet's treatment will be more effective than those sold in pet shops.

Serious illness

One day your cat might become very sick or have an accident and could be in a lot of pain. The vet may suggest that the kindest thing to do is to euthanize her: give her an injection that would cause her to die without pain. This decision may be hard to make, but it may be the kindest and most responsible thing you can do for your cat.

NEW KITTENS

Breeding season

There are certain times of the year when a female cat will be in heat, which means she can get pregnant. She may become restless and howl, calling for a mate. If you have a pedigree cat and you want her to have pure-bred kittens, you will need to find her a mate of the same breed and make sure she does not stray outdoors and mate with a domestic cat.

 Unless you are prepared to care for kittens, don't let your female cat outdoors while she is in heat, or she may come back pregnant!

Spaying and neutering

Before your kitten is six months old, you should decide whether to have it spayed or neutered: which means it can't have babies or get a female pregnant. This operation has many health benefits. Ask your vet for advice.

An unneutered male might run off to look for a mate, may get into fights with other males, and will spray a strong tom-cat smell everywhere. An unneutered female cat can have up to three pregnancies a year, with five or six babies in each litter!

Looking after your pregnant cat

If your cat is pregnant, take her to the vet to check that all is well. She will be pregnant for nine weeks. She will be hungrier than normal, so slowly increase the amount you feed her. She will need extra nutrients, so gradually switch her back to a complete kitten food.

Birth

Before she goes into labor, your cat will begin to search for somewhere to give birth, so keep cupboards and drawers shut! Put a few cardboard boxes lined with newspapers and blankets in quiet, warm places for her to choose from instead. Most cats have no trouble giving birth, and prefer to be left alone. Once they are born, the kittens will feed on their mother's milk.

She will need to eat a lot to produce enough milk. When the kittens are two days old, begin to stroke them gently with just one finger. At two weeks, you can lift each kitten out and hold it for a few minutes a day. At four weeks, the kittens will become more adventurous, so you can play freely with them. Enjoy this special time as they learn to explore the world!

Don't play with each kitten for more than five minutes at a time until they leave the box.

INDEX